# SHIPS

# BY CHRISTOPHER PICK

Galley Press

# CONTENTS

Introduction 4

Tall Ships 8

Modern Navies 22

Working Craft 29

Ocean Racing 44

Liners 47

Sport and Pleasure Craft 53

Index 64

*Left:* paddle-steamers such as this were for a long time the main means of transport on the Mississippi and Ohio Rivers.

# INTRODUCTION

The origins of ships are unknown. Possibly the idea of the raft, or another variation of a floating log, the dugout, was come upon merely by chance. We do know, however, that in the fourth millenium BC, in Egypt, seaworthy vessels were in existence, and archaeologists have discovered evidence of earlier boats.

The earliest *known* vessels were made of papyrus reed and, later, by about 1500 BC, of wood. Equipped with a single sail and oars, these boats ventured down the Red Sea and a little way along the east African coast; they also undertook Mediterranean voyages, reaching the coasts of modern Lebanon and Syria. Their construction was rudimentary, merely blocks of wood pegged together; the hull was weak, since it had no frame, and was held together by ropes stretched lengthwise round the hull and across it at bow and stern.

At about the same time, however, Minoan civilization in Crete developed an alternative, and far more satisfactory, method of ship-building, one that, in its basic principles at least, remained for as long as wooden ships were built. To the backbone of the vessel, the keel, were attached stem and stern posts, and ribs; then this skeleton was covered with planks laid lengthways, either overlapping or, as gradually became standard, flush. Once this standard pattern was established, refinements and modifications could be introduced and distinctions emerged between vessels used for trading and those used for war. The latter needed to be fast and easily manoeuvrable; these requirements were most efficiently provided by the galley, which was rowed by teams of oarsmen. The galley was relatively streamlined – 100 feet long and only 15 feet wide – and it was usually manned by two or three banks of oarsmen. Galleys fought the first recorded naval battle, at Salamis in 480 BC, when the Greek fleet routed the Persians. Galleys were equipped with sails, but these were never used in battle; to set sail was an admission of defeat.

Merchant vessels were commissioned and built to meet quite different requirements. A small crew was preferable to a large one because it was cheaper and because more space became available for cargo; nor were speed and manoeuvrability as important. The Phoenicians, the first great trading power of the Mediterranean, developed the round merchant ship, propelled by a large square sail. As first the Greeks and then the Romans grasped commercial predominance in the Mediterranean, earlier designs were adapted and improved. Roman grain ships, for instance, could carry 250 tons of cargo and 300 passengers.

Throughout this entire period – nearly four thousand years passed between the earliest Egyptian societies and the fall of the Roman Empire – sailing remained an uncertain business. Galleys were not built for long voyages; the square sails of merchant vessels were suitable only for sailing with the wind; and sailors, who had few means of determining their position at sea, tended to hug the coastline.

A glance at the quite separate development of sailing craft in Arabia and the Far East serves to remind us that the Mediterranean nations were by no means the first seafarers, or even the most advanced. The Chinese built junks, more seaworthy than anything in the west until the eighteenth century (they had an elementary rudder and could also sail close to the wind). The Arabs used a large triangular sail, which could be so trimmed that the boat could sail far closer to the wind than any vessel with a square sail.

Historians disagree about precisely when the triangular – or lateen, as it came to be known – sail reached the west; but certainly by the ninth century it was being used by Byzantine shipbuilders. Over the next centuries bigger and bigger vessels, known as nefs, were built.

---

On the right is a replica of the *Golden Hind*, Sir Francis Drake's famous galleon.

The Vikings journeyed as far south as Sicily and westward to America, in longboats – shallow, double-ended galleys equipped with both square sail and one bank of oars. As a fighting boat, the longship gained raised platforms at each end, known as 'castles'. For more peaceful purposes, the cog evolved, with more room gained for cargo by broadening the beam and deepening the draught.

From about the mid 15th century, the best features of the northern cog and the southern nef were combined. The result, the carrack, became the model on which all ships – both merchantmen and warships were based for the next three hundred years.

As specific demands for ships to do specific jobs were met, carracks were replaced by galleons, used for both military and mercantile purposes, then by ships of the line (so called because they entered battle in line) and by the East Indiamen, which plied between Europe, India and the East Indies.

Clippers, built to meet the 19th century's demand for speed, were introduced in the 1830s but their day was short-lived; the Suez Canal (which they were unable to use) cut sailing time to the East, steamships were becoming more reliable and, in the United States, the opening of the first transcontinental railway line meant that travellers no longer had to endure the laborious journey round Latin America.

Although the first steamships sailed in the early 19th century, it was a long time before their dominance was assured. The *Savannah* was the first steamship to make the Atlantic crossing, but she only got up steam for a total of 85 hours during a 25-day crossing. In 1838, the *Sirius* and then Brunel's *Great Western* both completed the trip entirely under steam (the former by resorting to the ship's furniture when the coal ran out). But

government and public were only convinced when the screw propellor had replaced paddles and ships were built of iron, (and towards the end of the century of steel). In 1859, the Royal Navy acknowledged this triumph when it laid down the *Warrior*, the first iron, armoured warship.

Now the pattern of the past repeated itself, and a range of improvements and new ideas were introduced. The end of the 19th century brought the era of the luxury liner; for a time too it brought a lack of respect for the sea, a belief that the new ships had overcome its dangers – an idea scotched by the sinking of the unsinkable *Titanic* in 1912. Firepower increased, and, as a result, faster, more manoeuvrable battleships, such as those of the Dreadnought class, were commissioned. In World War I, the two most powerful navies of the world sparred with each other just once, and that indecisively.

By the last years of World War II, the era of the battleship was coming to an end; many of the naval battles fought in the Pacific were air engagements and today the accent is on a faster and more flexible fleet of smaller vessels that can seek out and attack submarines, aircraft and guided missiles. Within little more than half a century, the great liners, supplanted by faster and cheaper air travel, were sailing to the scrapyards or, if they were lucky, were being converted to cruise ships. Today, trade and pleasure are the prime movers on the seas.

*Opposite:* the Swedish training schooner *Glada* is shown at start of the 1976 Tall Ships Race.

*Below:* amid the bustle of the Solent, one of England's busiest stretches of water, a hydrofoil passes under the stern of the Victorian steam yacht *Carola*.

# TALL SHIPS

For late twentieth-century man what more evocative
sight can there be than a tall ship under full sail? Seen
against the setting sun in the far distance, or at anchor in a
harbour, it outreaches in style and majesty all the craft
around it. Shown here is the German
sail training ship *Gorch Fock*.

Sad to say, it is today a rare privilege even to see a tall ship. By 1900 steam had gained its victory over sail, and very few tall ships have been built since then. Nowadays many of the survivors (like those illustrated here) serve as training ships, giving aspiring mariners a taste of the sea far saltier than most modern vessels can provide.

A number of the more important maritime trading nations operate sail training ships on which cadets, usually from the merchant marine, but sometimes from the navy as well, serve for a period of weeks or months. Though the days of sail are long past, it is generally held that such service before the mast – living in cramped quarters, undertaking all-night watches, sometimes literally battling with the elements – is a crucial part of any sailor's training.

Shown here are the *Dar Pomorza* (*right*), the *Sagres* (*below right*) and the *Gorch Fock* (*opposite*) from Poland, Portugal and Germany respectively.

The description square-rigged is always applied
to any vessel on which the main driving sails
are set from yards laced square to the mast,
no matter how many fore-and-aft sails it may
also be carrying. An example is the barque
*Amphitrite* shown here. (Barques and barquetines
may in fact carry far more fore-and-aft than
square sails.)

Until the late eighteenth century it was normal
practice to have square sails on all masts (this
was known as ship rig). Then fore-and-aft sails,
which could be handled by a smaller crew,
began to be introduced.

Barques such as the *Gorch Fock* (*left*) and the *Kruzenshtern* (*below left*) were but one step in sail's desperate attempt – doomed to failure as we now can tell – to stave off the takeover by steam. Further developments were the bar-quetine, on which only the foremast was square-rigged, and jackass barques, which had fore-and-aft sail on the lower mainmast and square sails on the top and topgallant masts.

The *Kruzenshtern* is a four-masted barque belonging to the Fishery Board of the USSR. Built in 1926 at Bremerhaven, Germany, she has 32 sails with a total area of 3700 square metres.

*Below:* is shown the Polish sail training ship *Dar Pornoza*. Built in 1909 in Hamburg and named *Prinz Eitel Friedrich*, she came into French possession in 1919 as part of the post-war reparations and ten years after that was bought by the Polish government. The necessary finance was donated by the people of Pomerania – hence the ship's name, which means 'Gift of Pomerania'. She made a round-the-world voyage in 1934 and 1935 and in 1968 sailed from her Baltic home round Europe to the Black Sea.

*Below:* the *Peking*, formerly named the *Arethusa II*, a four-masted barque, lies in dry dock for repairs to her hull before she is towed across the Atlantic. Dry docks provide the sole practical means of carrying out major repairs to a ship.

*Right:* crew members of the *Christian Radich* savour the prospect of an ocean voyage as their ship heads towards the open sea. The *Christian Radich* is a full-rigged training vessel owned by Norway and is in regular use for the training of cadets.

# Schooners

The *Juan Sebastian de Elanco*, a four-mast topsail schooner built for the Spanish navy in 1927. Schooners, among the fastest and most manoeuvrable of all sailing vessels, first became popular in the United States during the eighteenth century.

*Right* and *below* are shown the French sail-training ship *Bel Espoir II*, a three-masted schooner, and the *Falken*, a two-masted schooner. The original schooners, which date from the seventeenth century, were two-masted and had fore-and-aft sails. The topsail schooner, a later development, had a square topsail on the mainmast. The smaller schooners were used for coastal work, the larger versions, for oceanic journeys and for deep-sea fishing (one schooner was built with as many as seven masts).

*Opposite* is the *Seute Deern*, a ketch now operating as a training ship. The *Seute Deern* is a Baltic vessel. Used for fishing and as coastal freighters in the eighteenth and nineteenth centuries, the ketch carried fore-and-aft sails and had a crew of between four and eight men.

# MODERN NAVIES

In the last quarter of the twentieth century, navies are no
longer the potent symbol of a nation's military might that
they were only a few decades ago. Yet their role has not
vanished, for they not only guard the trading routes
of the world, but also, equipped with the latest sophisticated
weapons and missiles, form an important part of
national defence forces.

The development of naval technology has been astonishingly rapid during the twentieth century. As the great powers of Europe prepared for war in the early years of the century, the cry was for more battleships. No less than eight nations, significantly among them Germany, the USA and Japan, followed the Royal Navy's example and commissioned Dreadnoughts.

The USS *Arkansas*, (*right* – the illustration shows anti-aircraft guns being positioned) was laid down in January 1910 and completed in September 1912. She served in two World Wars, undergoing extensive alterations and a refit in 1925–27. She was finally expended during the Bikini atomic bomb tests in 1946.

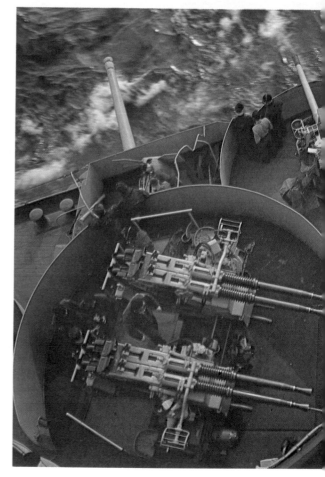

At the start of the Second World War, battleships still reigned supreme, and naval aircraft were principally used for reconnaissance purposes. By the end, aircraft carriers had become the major strike weapon and remained so during the first decades of peace. *Ark Royal* (*opposite top*) was the Royal Navy's last aircraft carrier. She carried only 30 fixed wing aircraft and nine helicopters. She was retired from the service in 1978.

Today, nuclear- and conventionally-powered submarines form an important part of many navies, together with a range of fast, manoeuvrable surface vessels supplied with sophisticated electronic equipment. Shown (*above*) is *Le Basque*, a French frigate.

*Above:* the Russian 'Kashin' class guided missile destroyer *Obraztsovy*. This class is the first in any of the world's navies to be powered entirely by gas turbines, which results in considerable speed benefits. The *Obraztsovy* has a complement of 300 and can reach 35 knots. Conversion work on the class, which was built from 1962 onwards, started in 1974 to equip them with up to date missiles.

*Opposite:* HMS *Tenacity* is the prototype of a new class of fast attack and patrol craft. Launched in 1969, and commissioned four years later, she is used on exercises and as a fishery protection vessel. Many such patrol boats are equipped with anti-ship missiles and their speed and agility make surprise attacks possible.

# WORKING CRAFT

It is all too easy to be seduced by the sea and its ships and to forget that there are vessels with a job to do. These pages show just a few of the spectacular variety of craft still engaged in maritime trade, that sure indicator of a sophisticated civilization.

*Left:* the *Ocean Venture* is shown in a lock on the Caledonian canal, Scotland. The Caledonian canal enables vessels to cross from coast to coast, avoiding the lengthy and dangerous voyage around Cape Wrath at the northern-most tip of Scotland.

Small trawlers and seiners operate from numerous ports in Scotland and the north of England, venturing forth for fish into what can be some of the most stormy waters in the world.

*Below:* a sloop on the Dutch Ijsselmeer, this shallow lake was formed when the Zuider Zee was enclosed in the 1930s. Sloops, single-masted fore-and-aft rigged boats, were originally small warships, three-masted and fully-rigged, with about 20 guns. More recently they have been used, like cutters, for offshore fishing.

*Below:* a harbour sampan, a small, light vessel used in the Far East as a house-boat and propelled by sculling with a single oar over the stern. Coastal sampans, which venture a little further out to sea, have a mast and sail like that on a junk.

*Opposite:* a junk is shown under sail near Hong Kong. Junks are probably the most ancient vessels still sailing the oceans. They were developed a thousand years ago or more, and are distinguished by their flat bottoms, high sterns and square bows; the two or three masts carry lugsails.
Junks have been used for practically every purpose – for fishing and trading, on rivers and the high seas, and also in battle. Their principal users have been the Chinese and Javanese.
In the eighteenth and nineteenth centuries, the largest junks were as big as the western square-rigged vessels, with a deadweight of as much as 4000 tons. Those still in use in East Asia today normally have a deadweight of about 500 tons.

*Opposite:* a sailing barge moves up an estuary on England's east coast. This is one of the centres of the fishing industry and an enormous variety of fishing and coastal sailing craft were developed here.

*Below:* an Indonesian fishing vessel is shown in the Java Sea. Since earliest times, man has gone to sea to take fish from the seemingly endless supply. Now, at least in certain parts of the world, the danger is that that supply will run out. Herring stocks in the North Sea and anchovy off the South American coast are two examples, and international cooperation is essential to prevent over-fishing.

*Right:* a lighter pushes its way through the winter ice of the Mittelland Canal, Germany. Lighters, flat-bottomed vessels like barges, are used for subsidiary journeys in international commerce and for transporting goods to and from ocean-going cargo vessels along inland water-ways. Some lighters are self-propelled, others are 'dumb' and have to be towed. A fairly recent innovation is the LASH (lighter aboard ship) which transports lighters themselves. Lighters are loaded on ocean-going vessels. Once their destination has been reached, they are unloaded to finish their journey.

*Below:* a Rhine barge, the *Santa Maria II*, loaded with timber, makes its way upstream.

*Opposite:* a sand and gravel boat is shown on the Rhine. The Rhine, perhaps western Europe's most important waterway, carries a wide variety of traffic. Already linked to the inland waterways' systems of France, Belgium and Holland – and to the North Sea via the Dortmund–Ems canal – the Rhine will by the early 1980s also have a connection with the Black Sea via the Rhine–Main–Danube Waterway. This waterway is already partly open and has transformed Nuremberg, 600 miles from the coast, into a thriving port.

*Above* is the tug *Helen McAllister*. Tugs are an indispensable and integral part of every harbour scene, towing both liners and cargo ships in and out of harbour. They are extremely powerful and manoeuvrable, as they need to be when guiding vessels many times their own size. The towing ropes are attached to the towing hook on the after end of the superstructure and to the bollards of the ship being towed. The raised bow and superstructure give good all-round visibility, essential in crowded harbours.

*Right:* the *Strazak*, a fire-fighting tug equipped with powerful pumps and water guns. A fire-fighting service is essential in every harbour.

*Opposite, top:* an inshore rescue launch speeds through a harbour. There are two main types of lifeboat, that used for inshore rescue and larger vessels suitable for deep-sea rescue in the severest conditions. Modern lifeboats are built of steel and are virtually unsinkable. Their equipment is highly sophisticated, often including a wide range of electronic and navigational aids, including radar, radio, echo-sounding equipment, intercom, line-throwing apparatus, breeches buoy, stretchers and other first-aid supplies. Inshore rescue launches are normally manned by a crew of two; deep sea boats have a complement of five.

*Below:* a pilot transfers from his launch to a Seagull lines ferry. Pilots conduct ocean-going vessels from the open sea into harbours and also through any particularly difficult channels: they must be taken on board passenger ships and are also compulsory for freighters unless the captain has a pilotage licence for that particular port.

*Opposite:* the Japanese-built oil-tanker *Univers Ireland.* Most tankers transport crude oil from the oil-fields to the consuming nations, though some have been built to handle liquid natural gas and a few are adapted to carry wine and molasses.

For many years tankers were relatively small and it was not until the 1960s that the super-tankers, the real giants of the oceans, began to roll down the slipways. Deadweights of 200,000 tons became common, the *Globtik Tokyo* reaching as many as 483,644 tons deadweight. Very Large Crude Carriers (VLCC) such as this are the largest mobile objects ever made by man. Engines, bridge and accommodation on tankers are at the stern, and the cargo is well separated from both stern and bows.

*Left:* a pleasure cruiser at Interlaken, Switzerland. Vessels such as these are an increasingly frequent sight on lakes and rivers throughout the western world, providing a comfortable, pleasant and relaxing excursion for holiday-makers.

*Below:* a roll-on roll-off (ro-ro) cross-channel ferry belonging to the Townsend-Thoresen line. Ro-ro vessels are now operating on numerous routes throughout the world and are rapidly replacing the old liner-type packets on to which cars were loaded by crane. The latest can carry as many as 350 cars and 1200 passengers: specially adapted versions for container lorries are also in operation.

# OCEAN RACING

## CLIPPER SHIPS

Clippers were the fastest of all sailing ships and throughout their brief but dramatic history they created record after record. At first the prizes went to the Americans. In 1851 the *Flying Cloud* completed the voyage from New York to San Francisco in 89 days, 21 hours. The *Lightning* ran 436 miles in twenty-four hours on her maiden voyage some three years later—a record never exceeded by another sailing vessel. Later, as the Gold Rush drew to a close and economic depression, and then the Civil War, hit American commerce, British clippers seized the lead. The real competition was to be the first to reach London with the new season's tea. In 1865 the *Fiery Cross* and the *Serica* put out from Foochow together, raced neck and neck up the English Channel and reached London Docks just one tide apart after a voyage of 107 days: the *Fiery Cross* was first. The following year, five clippers raced, setting sail within thirty hours of each other and 99 days later the three reached the London docks within two hours of one another.

This astonishing pace was maintained. In 1869, for instance, the *Sir Lancelot* needed only 84 days to reach the Lizard, at the far western tip of England, after leaving Foochow.

Perhaps the most famous clipper of all is the *Cutty Sark*, still on view at Greenwich in southeast London. Although her maiden voyage was to China, she soon moved to the Australia run. Here her average sailing time, $73\frac{3}{4}$ days, was not exceeded between 1874 and 1880. It has been estimated that her sail plan could produce as much as 3000 horsepower.

## LINER RACES

To win the Blue Riband was the aim of almost every trans-Atlantic line. The title, awarded to the ship achieving the fastest crossing of the Atlantic, was first gained in the 1840s, though it was not until 1933, when a silver trophy was made available, that it assumed a material form.

The first ship to hold the title was the *Acadia*, one of Samuel Cunard's first liners. She made the westward crossing in 1841 at an average speed of 10.76 knots. Her record eastbound was then beaten in 1851 by the Collins liner *Pacific* with a speed of 13 knots. Thereafter competition became increasingly fierce, as ship design improved and more and more lines were established. The record was set on no less than twelve occasions during the 1880s.

At the end of the nineteenth century, international rivalries entered the contest and Germany's North German Lloyd took the Riband in 1897 with *Kaiser Wilhelm der Grosse*, which averaged 22.35 knots. Great Britain retaliated with the *Mauretania*, launched in 1907. She held the record for over twenty years. Then came the German *Bremen* and *Europa* and the Italian *Rex*, which achieved 28.92 knots.

In the second half of the 1930s, the French *Normandie* and the British *Queen Mary* fought each other, the latter finally triumphing. The last liner to hold this much coveted award was the *United States*, which on her maiden voyage in July 1952 averaged 35.59 knots.

## SPEEDBOAT RECORDS

High speeds on water have always been a challenge, as much as those on land or in the air. In the history of the water speed record, the names of Malcolm and Donald Campbell, father and son, figure largely: Malcolm broke the record in 1937, 1938 and 1939 in *Bluebird* reaching 141.75mph in this last year, a speed not exceeded at his death nine years later. Then the record went to the United States, *Slo-Mo-Shun IV* reaching 160.32mph in 1950 and 178.49mph two years later. In 1955 Donald Campbell in *Bluebird* topped 200mph and nine years later achieved 276.33mph. In 1967, the same year in which the American *Hustler* took the record to 285.21mph, Donald Campbell was killed when *Bluebird* broke up on Coniston Water, in the English Lake District. He was travelling at 328mph at the time. The current record-holder is Ken Warby of Australia, who in October 1978 reached 319.627mph in his *Spirit of Australia*.

## THE LONERS

Although it is only in the last two decades that single-handed long distance voyages have become frequent and aroused so much media interest, contemporary yachtsmen are by no means pioneers. Alfred Johnson, an eastern seaboard fisherman, is the first known solo Atlantic yachtsman: he crossed to Pembrokeshire in Wales in 64 days in his 20ft dory *Centennial* on the anniversary of the American War of Independence in 1876. Having capsized 300 miles off the Irish coast, Johnson managed to right his boat but had to finish the voyage without food or dry clothes and bedding. Eighteen years later a Finn, Rudolph Frietsch, made the same crossing in a 40ft schooner, *Nina*, a remarkably large boat for one man to handle.

The challenge of the Atlantic mastered, the next target became a round-the-world voyage and the first man to achieve that, Joshua Slocum, set sail across the Atlantic from Boston, Massachusetts, on 24 April 1895. He sailed his boat, *Spray*, to Gibraltar, across the South Atlantic, through the Straits of Magellan and thence to Australia, on past the Cape of Good Hope, returning to Newport Rhode Island in June 1898.

During the first half of the twentieth century, the number of lone sailors increased, men of many different nationalities for many different reasons gladly meeting the physical and mental challenge of a solo voyage. It was not until 1960, however, that a new element—competition—came into play.

The first, and probably still the best-known single-handed race is the *Observer* newspaper's trans-Atlantic race, the OSTAR, which is run every four years. There were five entrants in the first race in 1960 when Francis Chichester won in *Gipsy Moth III* after completing the crossing in 40 days 11 hours. Since then more and more interest and competitors have been attracted by the race and the entry list has grown enormously. The most recent race, in 1976, was won by Frenchman Eric Tabarly in *Pen Duick VI*, whose voyage took only a few hours short of 24 days. Many of the most famous yachtsmen of the day have competed in this race—Alec Rose, 'Blondie' Hasler, Geoffrey Williams, Alain Colas and Bill Howell among them.

## YACHT RACES

Two of the most important international competitions in the yachting world are for the America's Cup and the Admiral's Cup.

The first contest for the America's Cup, at that time known as the Hundred Guinea Cup, was in 1851, when the 170 ton (measured tonnage) schooner *America* defeated 17 yachts in a race around the Isle of Wight. Ever since then the trophy has remained in American hands, despite some two dozen challenges from Great Britain, Canada, France, Australia and Sweden. The contest is decided on the best of seven races. Nowadays it is yachts of the International 12 Metre class that take part, rather than the large cutters, sloops and schooners of the pre-war days. The Admiral's Cup was inaugurated in 1957 and named after Sir Myles Wyatt, then Admiral of the Royal Ocean Racing Club. Yachts rating between 30 and 40ft under the International Offshore Rule take part in five races each, three inshore ones of about 30 miles each and two offshore. The latter includes the celebrated Fastnet Race, a course of 605 miles in the English Channel and Irish Sea. Countries that have won the cup are Great Britain (seven times), The United States (twice), Australia (once) and Germany (once). In 1971 the successful British Team was led by Edward Heath, at that time Prime Minister.

# LINERS

Liners in the last three decades have met and coped with unprecedented change. Once the normal means of international travel, they have lost out to the airplane as it became increasingly fast and increasingly cheap. But, not content to become a mere haven for the super-rich and the super-leisured, liners have found a new and successful role as cruise ships, providing relaxed and sophisticated vacations.

Three of today's luxury liners: *left*, P & O's *Sun Princess* under construction. P & O (the Peninsular and Oriental Steam Navigation Company) is one of the oldest liner companies. P & O developed the route to India, Hong Kong and Australia through the Mediterranean, then overland at Suez, and later through the Suez Canal, down the Red Sea and across the Indian Ocean. P & O still runs some passenger services, though much of its business comes from cruises.

*Opposite* is the *Canberra*, launched in 1961 and the largest ship ever built by P & O (it accommodates 2300 passengers). Its launching was a gesture of optimism towards the future and the liner has not failed the company's faith in it. She is still in service as a popular and luxurious cruise ship.

*Below*: the *Renaissance*, a 500-passenger liner which was launched in 1966 for the Compagnie Française.

*Right:* the *France*, with her famous winged funnels, is seen in Southampton Water. Built by the Compagnie Générale Transatlantique, better known to English-speaking travellers on both sides of the Atlantic as the French line, the *France* entered service in 1961, replacing the celebrated *Normandie*. Despite the unfavourable conditions of the 1960s for long-distance sea travel, the *France* ran at 80 per cent passenger capacity for that decade and into the early 1970s. (She could accommodate 407 first-class passengers, 1637 tourist-class.) But in 1974 the French government withdrew its operating subsidy, and the end was in sight – an end sadder and even more dramatic than might have been expected, for a strike committee representing the 1000 plus crew members who stood to lose their jobs took the ship over at the end of an Atlantic crossing and tried to keep the ship in service. Their efforts proved fruitless.

*Opposite:* the *Royal Viking Sky* is one of the three 22,000-ton sister ships operated on cruises by the Norwegian Royal Viking line.

*Left: Finnjet* is the latest in high-speed passenger and freight transport at sea. *Finnjet* entered service in 1977 on the Helsinki to Travemunde route and immediately reduced the time needed for the 1200-mile roundtrip from four to two days, spending a mere two hours in port between each voyage. Even in the worst of the winter weather *Finnjet* needs only three days for the roundtrip. 1500 passengers and 350 cars can be carried. (A reduction in the number of cars means that up to 34 lorries and 5 buses can also be accommodated.) *Finnjet* can reach 30 knots and is powered by two gas turbine engines.

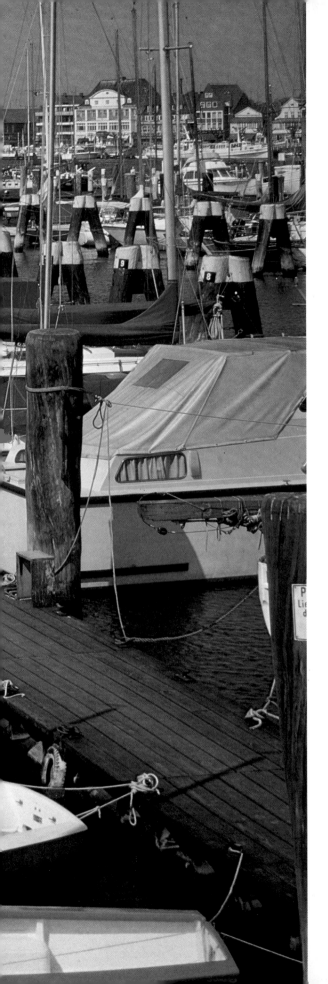

# SPORT AND PLEASURE CRAFT

With increasing prosperity and leisure, boating has found more and more enthusiasts. Its appeal, whether in a dinghy or sailing an ocean-going yacht, is easy to understand. Success depends to a large extent on the sailor's skills and seamanship: it is on a boat that modern man may hope to regain some sense of personal control in what can be an impersonal world.

*Opposite:* inshore racing off the English coast. Though it has become increasingly popular in recent years, yachting has a long and proud history. Both Charles II and James II in the seventeenth century were keen yachtsmen, as was William III, but it was not until the late eighteenth century, that the sport started to become organized. At first it was very much a rich man's hobby, but gradually smaller boats were evolved, within a more modest price range. By the first years of the twentieth century, international rules had been laid down, Olympic yachting beginning in 1908, and the sport was well on the way to its present success.

*Above:* yachts compete in a race during Cowes Week, the highpoint of every yachtsman's year. The races are held in August, near the Isle of Wight, off England's south coast (Cowes is the headquarters of the Yacht Squadron).

*Right:* Alec Rose returns home after his single-handed voyage round the world in the cutter *Lively Lady.* His trip, from Portsmouth, England, back to Portsmouth again via the Cape of Good Hope, Melbourne and Cape Horn, took just eleven months. Sir Alec (he was later knighted) is one of several deep-sea yachtsmen who have competed in the single-handed trans-Atlantic races and have then gone on to even more astonishing achievements.

Sailing dinghies moored alongside a jetty. Small dinghies such as these provide a relatively inexpensive, practical way of learning the fundamental skills of sailing on safe inland waters.

*Above*: the Oxford crew is shown during a recent Boat Race. The Boat Race – famous the world over as an English institution – was first rowed at Henley in 1829, and then in London annually from 1839. Its present course is $4\frac{1}{4}$ miles on the Thames in west London. In all, 125 races have been run, victory going to the light blues (Cambridge) on 68 occasions, to the dark blues (Oxford) 56 times. There has been one dead heat, in 1877. Each side has sunk, most recently Cambridge in 1978. In 1912 both boats sank and the race had to be re-run two days later.

For the spectators – undergraduates, graduates and the general public – the race is an enjoyable social occasion; for the oarsmen it is the culmination of months of exhausting, remorseless training and defeat must be as bitter as victory is glorious.

*Below left:* paddling across a river, one of the simplest and still one of the most pleasurable forms of boating.

Canoes are one of the oldest forms of water transport. They were used by the earliest travellers and fishermen, including the Indians of North America and the pioneer settlers of Canada. Nowadays, though they may provide less adventure, the drama remains, and canoeing, often over tricky shallows, as in this double canoe (*below*), is extremely popular.

*Overleaf:* Tony Williams drives in his Formula 1 powerboat *Olympus.* One of Britain's foremost powerboaters, Tony Williams was the European Formula 3 champion in 1977 and holds five national speed records and two world speed records. It was in this boat that he took the Formula 1 record at 113mph.

Powerboating has become increasingly popular in recent years but as in motor racing, the cost is so great that commercial sponsorship must be obtained. Among the more important competitions are the Harmsworth Cup and the American Gold Cup.

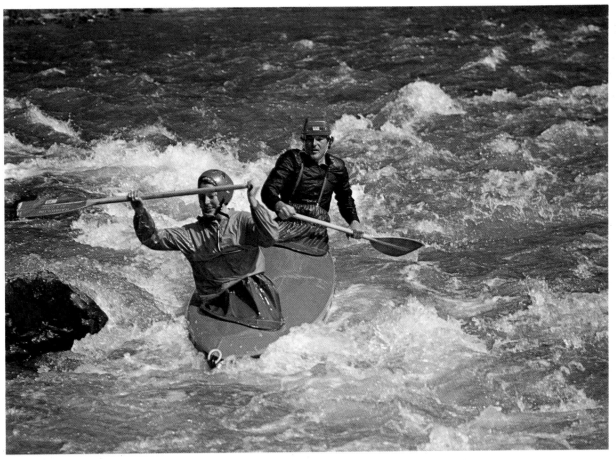

*Opposite top:* the Royal Yacht *Britannia* is shown at anchor. There have been royal yachts ever since the reign of Charles II (1660–85) but some monarchs have taken more interest in the sea than others. Queen Victoria (who had a house at Osborne, on the Isle of Wight near Cowes) was a particular enthusiast: she had no less than six royal yachts during her 63-year reign, all of them steam-powered. The present Royal Yacht, HMY *Britannia*, displaces 5769 tons and was launched in 1953. Her chief function is to act as a floating home and office for the monarch during royal visits both abroad and at home, providing much-needed relaxation between official duties.

*Opposite below* and *below:* the *Nareiros* and *La Belle Simone*, two luxury vessels of the kind that today can be owned and operated only by the very rich.

# INDEX

Italicized numbers refer to illustrations.

Acadia, 44
Admiral's Cup, 45
Aircraft carrier, 25
America, 45
American Gold Cup, 59
Ark Royal, 25
Atlantic, 16, 50

barque, 13, 16
barquetines, 13
battleship, 24, 25
Black Sea, 15, 36
Bluebird, 44
Blue Riband, 44
Blyth, Chay, 45
Boat Race, 58
Bremen, 44

Campbell, Malcolm and Donald, 44
Canberra, 49
canoe, 59
carrack, 6, 7
Centennial, 45
Chichester, Francis, 45
Columbus, Christopher, 7
cutter, 31
Cutty Sark, 44

Daily Express offshore race, 59
Daily Telegraph, round Britain
    race, 59
Dortmund–Ems Canal, 36
Dreadnoughts, 24

East India-men, 7
echo-sounding, 38
Europa, 44

Fiery Cross, 44
Finnjet, 51
Flying Cloud, 44
France, 50

galley, 4
gas turbine, 26, 50
Gipsy Moth III, 45
Globtik Tokyo, 40
guided missile destroyer, 26

Harmsworth Cup, 59
HMS Tenacity, 26
Hong Kong, 32
house-boat, 32
Hustler, 44
hydrofoil, 7

Ijsselmeer, 31
Isle of Wight, 54

Java Sea, 35
junk, 6, 32

Kaiser Wilhelm der Grosse, 44
ketch, 20

LASH, 36
lifeboat, 38
Lightning, 44
lighter, 36
liner, 47, 49
Lively Lady, 54

Mittelland Canal, 36
Navigator, the (Prince Henry
    of Portugal), 7
Normandie, 44, 50

oil-tanker, 40

Pacific, 44
paddle-steamers, 3
P & O (Peninsular and Oriental
    Steam Navigation Company), 49
Pen Duick VI, 45
pilot boat, 40
pleasure cruiser, 43
Portsmouth, 54
powerboat, 59

Queen Mary, 44
Queen Victoria, 63

Renaissance, 49
Rhine–Main Danube Waterway, 36
roll-on roll-off ferry, 43
Roman grain ships, 4
Rose, Alec, 54
Royal Viking Sky, 50
Royal Yacht Britannia, 63
Royal Yacht Squadron, 54

sailing barge, 35
sailing dinghies, 57
sail training ship, 8, 10, 15, 16, 20
sampan, 32
schooner, 19, 20
Serica, 44
Sir Lancelot, 44
Slo-Mo-Shun IV, 44
sloop, 31
Solent, the, 7
Spirit of Australia, 44
Spray, 45
steam yacht, 7
Sun Princess, 49

Taberly, Eric, 45
tall ship, 8, 10
Tall Ships Race, 1976, 7
Trawler, 31

Tug, 38

United States, 44
Univers Ireland, 40
USS Arkansas, 24

Very Large Crude Carriers,
    (VLCC), 40
Victorian steam yacht, 7
vikings, 6

William III, 54

Yachting, 54

Zuider Zee, 31

First published in 1979 by
Galley Press in association with
Cathay Books
59 Grosvenor Street, London W1

ISBN 0 86178 009 4

© 1979 Cathay Books

Produced by
Mandarin Publishers Limited
22a Westlands Road,
Quarry Bay, Hong Kong

Printed in Singapore.

PDO 79-153